POP CULTURE BIOS
SUPERSTARS

CARLY RAE

JEPSEN

CALL HER AMAZING

NADIA HIGGINS

Lerner Publications Company

MINNEAPOLIS

Lerner Publications Company
A division of Lerner Publishing Group, Inc.
241 First Avenue North
Minneapolis, MN 55401 U.S.A.

Website address: www.lernerbooks.com

Library of Congress Cataloging-in-Publication Data

Higgins, Nadia.
        Carly Rae Jepsen : call her amazing / by Nadia Higgins.
            p.   cm. — (Pop culture bios: superstars)
        Includes index.
        ISBN 978–1–4677–1306–1 (lib. bdg. : alk. paper)
        ISBN 978–1–4677–1768–7 (eBook)
        1. Jepsen, Carly Rae, 1985- —Juvenile literature. 2.
    Singers—Canada—Biography—Juvenile literature. I. Title.
    ML3930.J47H54 2014
    782.42164092—dc23 [B]   2013002318

Manufactured in the United States of America
1 – BP – 7/15/13

INTRODUCTION

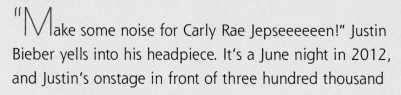

"Make some noise for Carly Rae Jepseeeeeen!" Justin Bieber yells into his headpiece. It's a June night in 2012, and Justin's onstage in front of three hundred thousand people. They've packed an outdoor square in Mexico City.

Justin walks over and welcomes Carly with a bear hug. She floats upstage in a white summer dress. "Hello!" she calls out. From up here, the crowd looks like swirling shadows and lights.

"A lot of people, right?" Justin says to her, smiling. He knows Carly has never performed in front of a crowd this size. Not even close.

Carly heads to a press event in Mexico City in June 2012.

The violins take off. Next thing she knows, Carly's singing her smash hit, "Call Me Maybe." She's wearing her huge, sweet grin. She's pumping her arms. She's twirling, flashing neon hot pants under her skirt.

But something's wrong. For the first time since the age of seven, this natural-born performer is *nervous.* And can you blame her? Her life lately has read like a Cinderella fairy tale on fast-forward. Four months ago, nobody had heard of her outside of Canada. Now she's the Biebs' surprise special guest!

Thousands of fans pack Zócalo Square in Mexico City to see Carly sing with Justin Bieber in June 2012.

A little way in, Carly loses her breath. She thinks she's about to fail. But there's no striking clock in *this* fairy tale. She looks up at the crowd. All three hundred thousand fans are filling in for her, word for word.

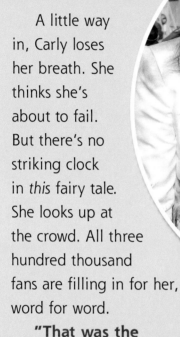

Carly poses for a photo with Justin Bieber in July 2012.

"That was the moment I knew," Carly later spilled to *Cosmopolitan.* She knew she'd made it. She knew she was ready for whatever was coming next.

CHAPTER ONE

A TOTAL NATURAL

Carly was born in the town of
Mission in western Canada.

Sometimes Carly Rae Jepsen gets freaked out by being famous. So she does a special trick. The pop star reminds herself that she is just "a music geek." It doesn't matter how many hits she makes. "The creative process is the same," she says. Carly loves singing—and she always has.

Pitch Perfect

Carly Rae Jepsen was born on November 21, 1985, in the town of Mission, British Columbia, in western Canada. Carly is the middle kid. She has an older brother, Colin, and a little sister, Katie.

Carly's parents divorced early on. Looking back, Carly talks fondly of growing up in two houses. Her father and mother are both teachers. So are her stepparents. Carly calls her family the reason for her success. **"Music was the way I connected with everyone, and my family encouraged that in me,"** she says.

Carly was one of those happy kids who was always singing. Her father remembers the day he realized she sang perfectly on key. She was only three years old!

When Carly was little, her father would sing her to sleep with James Taylor songs. That folk artist (LEFT) still gives her warm fuzzies. For Christmas 2012, Carly bought her dad his dream guitar. It's the same kind James Taylor plays!

Pirate Princess

When Carly was seven, she was getting ready for her stage debut at a local talent contest. She ran to her closet to get her frilly pink dress. But Carly couldn't reach the top. So she yanked on the bottom of the dress, until…*boing!* The hanger popped off and scratched her eyeball.

STAGE DEBUT = a person's very first time performing in public

That night, Carly performed "Beauty and the Beast" in her pink dress—and an eye patch. At first, she was nervous. By the end, though, the stage felt like home. **"I knew I wanted to spend my life doing that from that moment on,"** Carly dished to MTV.

A Gleek before Her Time

In high school, everybody knew where to find Carly. She was usually in rehearsal. Carly was super into musical theater back then. She played starring roles in *Annie*, *Grease*, and *The Wiz*, to name a few.

The musical *Grease* was a popular film as well as a stage production.

WANDER WOMAN

When she was little, Carly told her mom that she wanted to live in hotels when she grew up. (And now...well, she kind of does.) She's also gone on record as saying that she loves sleeping overnight on buses.

Carly moved to Victoria, British Columbia, to work on her performing.

When Carly was seventeen, she went to the Canadian College of Performing Arts in nearby Victoria. She spent a year training to be a Broadway star. Looking back, she laughs at her attempts to learn ballet and tap. Those types of dance just weren't her strong suit. She also memorized famous speeches from plays. She sang plenty of scales too.

SCALE =
a set of musical notes that go up and down in predictable ways

Around this time, Carly got a present that would change her life. It was her very first guitar. She started writing songs right away. And she hasn't stopped since.

WORST NICKNAME EVER

Growing up, Carly's family called her Raymond as a joke ('cuz her middle name is Rae—get it?). Carly didn't really mind. Then her stepmother got a dog and named it Raymond too. That was the end of Carly's nickname!

GROWING AS AN ARTIST

Carly wanted to write and perform her own music. Her goal wasn't to be famous. It was just to do what she loved—and make the rent.

Carly moved to the city of Vancouver. For the next several years, she worked in coffee shops and waited tables. She took any chance she could to perform.

One day, she was looking through newspaper listings for music jobs. She saw that a swing band was looking for a saxophone player. She didn't play the sax, but so what? She talked the band into letting her sing for them anyway. They hired her as their lead singer (of course!).

SWING =
a kind of old-fashioned music with upbeat rhythms and horn instruments

A Perfect Third

Meanwhile, Carly's old high school drama teacher was on her case. Why wouldn't Carly try out for *Canadian Idol*? Her former teacher thought this TV talent show would be perfect for her! The instructor told her, "Don't decide your path. Let it decide you."

Finally, in 2007, Carly agreed. She grabbed her guitar, stepped into one of her many pairs of heels, and headed off to audition.

The rule was that you had to sing a cover. But Carly wanted to sing one of her own songs. So she did. The judges were so wowed they forgot the rules anyway. One of them gushed that Carly was an "absolute bona fide total star"!

Carly came in third on *Canadian Idol.* She was stoked! The way she saw it, every week she didn't lose was a bonus. Looking back, she's relieved she got third place. She got publicity without being tied down to a winner's contract. That might have forced her to sing songs she didn't choose herself.

COVER =
a performance of a song that has already been done by another artist

PUBLICITY =
positive attention from the media in the form of articles, TV spots, etc.

SHOE LOVE

Carly says she is crazy about shoes. Since she's only five feet two, she wears heels most often. She even carries a separate suitcase just for shoes when she travels!

On Her Way

Canadian Idol was Carly's first big break. Soon she got a deal with a Canadian label and started working on her first album. *Tug of War* came out in September 2008. This folkie collection established Carly as a serious artist. Two of her songs, "Tug of War" and "Bucket," became hits in Canada.

Carly performs the song "Sour Candy" from the album *Tug of War* in 2010. Next to her is singer and producer Josh Ramsay, who produced "Call Me Maybe" the next year.

For the next few years, Carly toured Canada building her fan base. Her "tour bus" was a minivan. She set up and ran her own merch table. She just hoped that nobody would steal her T-shirts while she was onstage!

Getting Curious

Meanwhile, Carly's sound was changing. She was drawn to the energy of pop. By fall 2011, Carly was getting ready to release an EP. It was called *Curiosity*, to reflect her changing musical mood.

In September, her label released a single from her EP, "Call Me Maybe." It was a song Carly pulled together in just five days!

CARLY RAE JEPSEN
Call Me Maybe

LYRICS =
words to a song

The lyrics and music came easily to her—plus, her guitarist and other friends happily pitched in to help her write it.

By December, Carly's song was all over Canadian radio. And Justin Bieber was coming home to Canada for Christmas any day…

SO HAS SHE EVER?

"Call Me Maybe" is about a girl who gives a cute stranger her number. Has Carly ever done that? No way! She's too shy. She met her current beau, musician Matthew Koma, through a friend. The couple (RIGHT) got together in August 2012. These days they are still going strong.

CHAPTER THREE

AN AMAZING YEAR

In late December 2011, Carly's sister called her up screaming. Had Carly heard the news? Justin Bieber had tweeted about her! The Biebs had written: "Call Me Maybe by Carly Rae Jepsen is possibly the catchiest song I've ever heard lol." Carly and her little sis couldn't believe it!

Then, in February 2012, Justin, Selena Gomez, and Ashley Tisdale made a video with a bunch of friends. The celebs are having a total blast. They're bopping around in fake mustaches. They're juggling in fur hats. They're holding banana telephones—while lip-synching to "Call Me Maybe." The video went instantly viral. It got one million views in the first twenty-four hours alone!

LIP-SYNCHING =
mouthing the words
to a song

Selena Gomez (LEFT) and Ashley Tisdale also loved Carly's song!

Deep Breaths Required

Later that month, Carly wrote in her blog, "I can't explain last week to you. **Flights, photos, interviews and the constant worry that it's all too good to be true.** It has required deep breaths. With me now...1,2,3...and out, 1,2,3."

That week, Carly had found herself in Los Angeles signing a deal with Justin's label, School Boy Records. She remembers sitting at a table with twenty-six music professionals. Carly wouldn't have to worry about running her own merch table anymore! At the same time, her life was about to become crazy busy. She was booked solid with performances and media events.

Jesse Giddings (FRONT LEFT) interviews Carly on the Canadian music network MuchMusic in February 2012.

The Craze Begins

Meanwhile, the whole world was gaga over "Call Me Maybe." By early June, it was No. 1 on U.S. pop charts. (Eventually, it would go to the top in thirty-seven countries. It also got the most iTunes downloads of 2012.)

Carly performs at the Billboard Music Awards on May 20, 2012.

But "Call Me Maybe" wasn't just the best earworm in years. It inspired fans to get their goofy on! Like Justin and Co., they whipped out their cameras and grooved. By early July, fans had posted more than sixty-three thousand "Call Me Maybe" covers on YouTube.

CARLY'S FAVS

Drink: tea with honey (Carly keeps honey packets in her purse.)
Food: sushi (She makes it herself.)
Book: *The Hunger Games* (She's Team Peeta.)
Game: chess
Celebrity crush: Ryan Gosling

On March 2, 2012, Carly went to Justin's star-studded birthday bash. At first, she was so freaked out she just stood there. A security guard actually had to tell her to go in and join the party. She did—and sang Justin's favorite song too.

Pressure's On

But Carly's life wasn't 100 percent bummer-free. Travel is one of Carly's all-time favs. Still, enough is enough. Some days she found herself in three different cities. She missed her family.

Also, Carly was pretty sure that someone was stealing personal photos from her computer. (She would be proven right. In December 2012, Vancouver police brought charges against a hacker.)

Carly spends a lot of time traveling for concerts and interviews.

Then, in July, some creeper posted fake nude photos of her on the Web. Luckily, Carly's body double came forward and fessed up right away.

Most of all, Carly couldn't stop worrying that this was all too good to be true. It didn't help that some people were calling her a one-hit wonder. Carly was busy working on her next album. That kind of pressure was *not* helpful. But "Good Time," her new single with Owl City, came out in July. And luckily, it went straight to the top ten.

ONE-HIT WONDER = an artist who comes up with just one famous song

ASK CARLY

On boys: "My philosophy is to play no games. I think the sooner you lead with your heart, the better."

Career advice: "You should knock on every door and not turn your nose up at any opportunity, because you never know what's going to work."

Keepin' it real: "I don't want to make the goal having No. 1s. I try not to feel pressure except to make quality music."

Kiss and Beyond

In September, *Kiss* came out. The pop album is all about love. But the songs aren't necessarily from Carly's own life, she insists. Critics gave *Kiss* mixed reviews, but not her fans. They couldn't stop rocking to its dancy beats and catchy hooks.

That month, Carly also began opening for Justin's Believe tour. No more stage nerves for her! She became a pro at playing in front of huge crowds.

Carly takes to the stage during Justin Bieber's Believe tour in October 2012.

What's next for Carly? She hopes to sell out her own world tour soon. And of course, she's always writing music. But if her amazing year has taught her anything, it's that you never know what's coming. And that's awesome. As Carly revealed to E! Entertainment, **"I love not knowing where I'm going."**

CARLY
PICS!

Carly performs with Owl City (LEFT) on the *Today* show on August 23, 2012.

Carly crowd surfs during a concert in Frankfurt, Germany.

SOURCE NOTES

5   *Carly Rae Jepsen—Call Me Maybe—en Mexico City Zocalo*, YouTube video, 2:11, posted by Cesar spears, November 15, 2012, http://www.youtube.com/watch?feature=player_embedded&v=PvP9IpaSqIo#! (January 16, 2013).

5   Ibid.

5   Ibid.

7   Ky Henderson, "Carly Rae Jepsen Is Our January Cover Girl!" *Cosmopolitan*, 2013, http://www.cosmopolitan.com/celebrity/exclusive/carly-rae-jepsen-january-cover (January 16, 2013).

9   Jocelyn Vena, "Carly Rae Jepsen Rocked an Eye Patch Before She 'Made It': Watch a Sneak Peek!" *MTV*, December 20, 2012, http://www.mtv.com/news/articles/1699259/carly-rae-jepsen-this-is-how-i-made-it-sneak-peek.jhtml (January 16, 2013).

9   Jason Lipshutz, "Dialed In," *Billboard*, June 30, 2012, 18.

9   "About Carly Rae Jepsen," Carly Rae Jepsen, 2012, http://www.carlyraemusic.com/biography/ (January 16, 2013).

11   Vena, "Carly Rae Jepsen Rocked an Eye Patch."

15   "About Carly Rae Jepsen," Carly Rae Jepsen.

16   *Carly Rae Jepsen—Audition*, YouTube video, posted by pistolsaf, October 7, 2007, http://www.youtube.com/watch?v=V458He7UYSM (January 16, 2013).

21   Justin Bieber, Twitter, posted on December 30, 2011.

22   "Dear You," Carly Rae Jepsen, February 22, 2012, http://www.carlyraemusic.com/blog-carly-rae-jepsen/ (January 16, 2013).

25   Carlos Greer, "Meet 'Call Me Maybe' Singer . . . Carly Rae Jepsen," *People*, May 21, 2012, 48.

25   Henderson, "Carly Rae Jepsen."

25   *Carly Rae Jepsen part 2*, YouTube video, 6:39, posted by saidamahoney, September 19, 2012, http://www.youtube.com/watch?v=u6qOlr1rvuE (January 16, 2013).

27   *Carly Rae Jepsen Interview [Extended]*, YouTube video, 8:54, posted by GlobalToronto, July 12, 2012, http://www.youtube.com/watch?v=KxX1k32X1Hw (January 16, 2013).

MORE CARLY INFO

Can-Dos with Carly Rae Jepsen
http://www.youtube.com/watch?v=JBQmb-zfobE
Can Carly whistle? Juggle? Lick her own elbow? Carly calls this funny interview the "weirdest" one she's ever done.

Carly Rae Jepsen
http://www.carlyraemusic.com
Find personal details you won't see anywhere else in Carly's bio. This official site is also the best place to find Carly's upcoming tour schedule and to see her latest merch.

Higgins, Nadia. *Justin Bieber: Pop and R & B Idol*. Minneapolis: Lerner Publications Company, 2013. Justin's rise to fame is even more unlikely than Carly's. Read the surprising life story of the guy who made it all happen for her.

Pop Dust Supercut: Carly Rae Jepsen's "Call Me Maybe"
http://www.youtube.com/watch?v=QYWDySIzfFU
Check out this hilarious mash-up of the best seventy-five covers of Carly's hit.

INDEX

The images in this book are used with the permission of: © Bill McCay/WireImage/Getty Images, pp. 2, 28 (top left); Dominic Chan/WENN.com/Newscom, pp. 3 (top), 8 (top), 13, 17; © John Barrett/Globe Photos/ImageCollect, pp. 3 (bottom), 20 (bottom left); © Michael Tran/FilmMagic/Getty Images, p. 4 (top left); © Dennis Van Tine/starmaxinc.com/ImageCollect, p. 4 (top right); © Trisha Leeper/WireImage/Getty Images, p. 4 (bottom); Carlos Tischler/Rex/Rex USA, p. 5; © Yadin Xolalpa/El Universal/ZUMAPRESS, p. 6; © Kevin Mazur/WireImage/Getty Images, pp. 7, 29 (bottom left); © The British Columbia Collection/Alamy, p. 8 (bottom); © Michael Riley/Dreamstime.com, p. 10; © Globe-Photos/ImageCollect, p. 11; © Pete Ryan/National Geographic/Getty Images, p. 12; © George Pimentel/WireImage/Getty Images, p. 14 (bottom); Paul Darrow/REUTERS/Newscom, p. 14 (top); © Byron Purvis/AdMedia/ImageCollect, pp. 16, 20 (bottom right); © Todd Strand/Independent Picture Service, p. 18; © Christopher Polk/Getty Images for NARAS, p. 19; © Moses Robinson/Getty Images, p. 20 (top); © Acepixs/ImageCollect, p. 21 (top left); © John Shearer/KCA2012/Getty Images for KCA, p. 21 (bottom right); © Sonia Recchia/WireImage/Getty Images, p. 22; © Christopher Polk/Billboards2012/Getty Images for ABC, p. 23; © Splash News/Corbis, p. 24; © Jason Squires/WireImage/Getty Images, p. 26; © Mike Marsland/WireImage/Getty Images, p. 28 (right); Charles Sykes/Invision/AP, p. 28 (bottom); © Michael Stewart/WireImage/Getty Images, p. 29 (top left); © Jason LaVeris/FilmMagic/Getty Images, p. 29 (top center); © Kevan Brooks/AdMedia/ImageCollect, p. 29 (right).

Front Cover: © StarMaxWorldwide/ImageCollect (main); © George Pimentel/WireImage/Getty Images (inset).
Back Cover: © Michael Stewart/WireImage/Getty Images.

Main body text set in Shannon Std Book 12/18.
Typeface provided by Monotype Typography.